G[uided]
Medit[ation]
Kundalini
Awakening

Align Your Chakras, Awaken Your

Third Eye, Become More

Confident, Find Inner Peace, and

Heal Your Soul

By

Kaizen Mindfulness Meditations

Table of Contents

I: Gather Your Energy

As you prepare yourself for this meditation of kundalini awakening, come to a comfortable position. Whether it's a seated, standing, or reclined position, gather yourself and collect your energy for this moment. Allow yourself to slow down your active, everyday self. Allow yourself to connect with the deeper and more cosmic energy of your soul. You'll have to calm down that everyday self, of course, before you can make any giant steps. So, let's begin there.

In your comfortable position, close your eyes gently. Don't tightly shut them, just let gravity pull them down and let yourself look at nothing as they come to close. In that dark space behind your eyes, let your imagination take control. Let your thoughts come and go at first and get a sense for their speed, their themes, their focus. Let any emotions filling you up simply be present and as you're able to, let yourself come to terms with that presence. Look around in this space behind your eyes and notice what's going on inside you. Go past just this mental realm too, go down slowly through your whole body to give a systems check to yourself.

Move from your mind to your nose, your mouth, and your throat. Do you feel any congestion or pain here? Any bad feeling or simply free flow? Move down then to your shoulders, your chest, your heart, and your lungs. What's going on deep within? Is there any distracting tension? Do you have any pain or discomfort here? Any excitement or over-working? Or simply free flow? Move down again and out to your arms. Are they sore or tight or stiff, or do you hardly feel them hanging there? Are your hands numb or ready for action? Down to your stomach, your abdomen, and your hips. Are things okay here? Do you feel any tension or discomfort, perhaps from indigestion or malnutrition in some way? And even lower, in your pubic and genital region, how are things feeling? Are you comfortable with yourself here or do you have traumas attached that aren't able to be discussed yet? In your legs and your feet, how are things flowing here?

As you conduct this internal assessment of your body, try your best to breathe deeply and as evenly as possible. Try not to hold your breath at any time, but if you happen to do so, note which area of the body you happen to be scanning at the time and think, too, of what that link could mean for your overall health. Your innate pattern of breathing has a lot to say about what's going on deep within. Do you breathe deeply and evenly always or do you have issues with holding your breath and not even knowing it? As with a bit earlier, do you hold your breath only when you encounter certain problems or when you think about certain things? Try to learn more about yourself through this bodily assessment – through your breathing flow, your tensions, and your painful places. Look deep within and prepare yourself for what's to come.

With your eyes closed and your breathing sure and steady, with your internal state in check and your goals on the meditation at hand, you must now establish your center. When you investigated those bodily spaces before, you likely felt how your consciousness can move to different regions of your body at your command. You hopefully felt how you can bring all of your attention to your stomach area with practice, or to your throat or your third eye and imagination space. In this case, you'll bring all your energy and attention into a space you'll define as your "center."

Your center can be wherever you feel it should be and for now, let that central place come to you intuitively. For you, is it in that behind-the-eyes space? Or is it in your heart? Your diaphragm? Your gut? Where do you feel your energy circulating around as if it was an energetic vortex within you? Wherever your consciousness is pulled, let this space be your "center" for now and then breathe into that space. Breathe deeply, giving energy and life to this area, dissolving any tension and letting any thoughts or feelings about it come and go like mist evaporating in the sun.

Breathe attentively and let your inner awareness come to life.

What you're noticing when you built up your center and when you breathe life into your body is your kundalini. What you're noticing when you quiet your thoughts and still your mind to a peaceful emptiness is your kundalini, too. The cosmic energy that pervades daily life is kundalini and it lives reflected within you and within me, too. Within all of us, this uncoiled energy waits to be awakened so it can dance with the universe around it and when you look deeply into yourself, breathing as consciously as possible, you allow the universal energy within yourself to arise and acknowledge *itself*.

When you spent time noticing each realm of your body, you performed important work related to the healing of your kundalini energy. Sometimes, this energy can become corrupted by imbalances within us. Sometimes, we can lose touch with our kundalini entirely by distractions in everyday life, but the kundalini still rests in wait, coiled up in the pits of our stomachs, curled up around the seats of our souls.

When you did that energetic assessment earlier, whatever areas you felt in pain or tension will likely later (or now) be areas of imbalance, where blockages are keeping your kundalini energy from flowing freely. As we move forward, what you noticed then will demand that you grow strong enough to heal that weakness in the future and you needn't be overwhelmed or afraid. Simply know this healing is coming. The abilities you need to succeed are readily housed deep in your core and you wouldn't be here if you weren't equipped for the ride.

II: On the Kundalini

The origins of studies on the kundalini come from times as early as 1000 BC in Hindu tradition, where historical records indicate the importance of the energy science and the spiritual philosophy behind this particular aspect of creation. According to the original studies, kundalini refers to the spiritual energy we all contain that's located at the base of our spines. This spiritual energy itself is referred to as Shakti, but kundalini is the great potential all living beings have to become aligned with that godly, universal presence.

For these early practitioners – and for kundalini scholars, students, and practitioners today – the kundalini was described as snake-like. It was physically described as a serpent and the actions it completed as a vessel of energy within a living body were then commented on in theme. That coiled up energy at the base of the spine would unravel and dance like a charmed snake through the basic energy wheels of the living body and then the snake would reach the crown of the body and turn back down, establishing a flowing serpentine motion through the body, hitting every major internal energy center on the ways up and down in order to trigger awakening.

Literally, the word "kundalini" derives from a Sanskrit word that hints at something that's small and coiled up — in this case, the presence of "God" or source energy within all living things. Metaphysically and spiritually, kundalini suggests that we can unlock our godly potential and come to live purer lives through both knowledge and guided meditation. The knowledge required first relates to some of the smallest and most important vehicles of energy in our bodies. First things first, the knowledge required necessitates an understanding of chakras.

As you breathe deeply at this moment and feel centered in your body, ready to learn and grow with this meditation, remember those realms of the body we walked through before. Recall those places of tension, the place of free flow, and the sensation of finding your "center." What we were really doing in those moments was taking a journey down through your chakras to assess the general state of things.

As we move forward with this meditation, keep this even pace of breathing and visualize along with the information being shared with you. In your body, there are seven places where energy is pushed through your body. These seven places relate to seven glands of the human body – those small and important energy vehicles in the body – and seven energetic "chakras." Literally, chakra means a wheel or disk that directs the flow of energy. Each of these chakras is spaced at different parts of the body, but all along the vertical line of the spine. Starting from the base and moving up, these energy wheels help us process emotional and mental complexities related to these bodily spaces and they work to keep the overall vibration of the body flowing in harmonious balance.

The kundalini reflects on how the movement through your chakras is going. It asks how things are going for you deep within and it posits that health problems or imbalances of other sorts easily arise when things are not going well but remain clearly avoided. The kundalini requires a degree of self-awareness, to that effect, although the kundalini and its potential still exists within every living body. The more cognizant and driven you are in your practice, however, the better.

When you meditate on the kundalini, it awakens bit by bit. When you meditate *to awaken* the kundalini, it responds immediately. Your coiled-up snake then shivers awake and quivers into the warmth and starts going about its business with a little more urgency. As the snake starts to move, it will begin at the base of your spine and move first through your Root Chakra which is all about survival and links to the color red. As it moves through your Root Chakra, it will provide healing and balancing godly energy to your feelings about sex, intimacy, and overall security.

The snake will then move up into your Sacral Chakra, which is all about creativity and links to the color orange. The Sacral Chakra will experience the blessings of this rising snake through increased inspiration, vehicles to let out their creativity, and affirmations that they're supported and loved. Moving onwards, the snake will go through your Solar Plexus Chakra, which is all about willpower and links to the color yellow. As the serpent moves through this chakra, it will remind you how to say no and what's worth saying yes to.

Moving up to the Heart Chakra, which is all about love and devotion linking to the color green, the snake will make you question your relationship to *love* itself as well as what might be blocking your ability to love. As the snake moves on upwards, it encounters the Throat Chakra, which is about communication and links to the color of light blue. Here, the snake will encourage you to examine how your words are used and what their consequences are. Then, the snake moves through the Third-Eye Chakra, which is about seeing beyond sight and links to the color of dark or indigo blue. In this region, the snake's movement helps you realize what you might have been missing or unintentionally blind to.

Finally, the snake will move up and through the Crown Chakra, which is all about connecting to the higher self and links to the color purple. In this sphere, the serpent helps you align your life with your greatest potential and opens you up to messages and gifts from the universe. After the snake gets to the top, however, it turns right back down and goes through them all again before going right back up to the top. The kundalini within us is relentless when we invite its awakening. It wants us to open up and connect with the source, with the divine.

The kundalini runs on your trust, devotion, and hope. It runs on your commitment and determination too, for your commitment to these meditations will certainly help your progress along more than would be the case without them.

The kundalini works to get your energy flowing and then you get to see what falls in place around that healed-up core. Through practice, conscious breathing, and the desire to access your higher awareness, in time you *will* awaken your kundalini and begin on your path to enlightenment.

III: Your Inner Truth

Look back now on what you noticed before with your trouble spot (or spots!) and imagine that you can see that area (or areas) surrounded by the color of the nearest chakra. If you're having issues with your reproductive area, (desires to have children without the ability to do so or recent or long-past trauma, etc.) then envision that you can see deep beneath the skin to the trouble spot and the area is surrounded in a warm, red bathing light. If you're having issues with your heart – not feeling loved or feeling like you have so much to give but no one to take it, etc. – look deep into your heart and see that area bathed in warm, forest green light. You get the picture.

Find that trouble spot and look deep within. Look directly at it now, with the intention of healing. Breathe consciously — slowly, deeply, quietly, and constantly. Breathe into that space and see that colored light glow brighter. Imagine that you can feel the kundalini at your core – the snake that lives along your spine – starting to move and wiggle its way to the same place that holds your attention. As it moves upwards and downwards at a steady pace, it hits this trouble spot twice each cycle, once on the way up and once on the way down. With this constant attention and healing interaction, visualize that the light behind your pain starts to fade from bright red, blue, green, or whatever to pure and simple white.

Look into that space of turmoil and see your attachments to it fade as the light changes tones. Look deeply and realize that what so many people have said across time is true — you can't rush perfection. Since you know what you want in terms of healing, let's have you try something new rather than angry hoping or pressured affirmations. Let's have you make yourself as emotionally neutral as possible as the kundalini snake keeps making its rounds. Let's have you become quiet on the inside, less distracted, and fully open for anything. Let's get that snake moving and then we'll learn to vocalize what you really want.

While you're looking deep inside yourself still, with neutral feeling towards your body and your trouble spot(s) now, test yourself. Feel this serpent move over your trouble spot and you know that space is being purified, pumped-through with godly or source energy. Trust that healing is happening without you trying to force it. Now, with strong posture, internal consciousness, and a positive attitude about healing (but no emotions otherwise), begin a chant of your choice.

When you think of what you want for your awakening, is it purely bodily? Are you looking for joint healing, glandular healing, or otherwise? Or is it purely spiritual? Are you hoping for an increased connection to the divine and further gifts to amp up that relationship? Is it a mix of the two, perhaps? When you think of what you want for your kundalini awakening, there must be some words that come to mind. As you complete this visualization with the snake and your trouble spots, begin to speak aloud these words until they become like a chant.

For kundalini energy raising, chanting works incredibly powerfully. When you repeat over and over what your soul truly needs, the universe can't help but respond, but also, in these meditative moments with this type of repetitive vocal practice, your kundalini energy will find itself awakened all that much easier because you can put words to your hopes – because you've aligned your voice with the goals of your higher self. That alignment activates so much potential.

If you need to take a moment before moving on to brainstorm a little more direction for your kundalini awakening, that's absolutely understandable. In all actuality, it's probably a smart move to define your goals and check them against your higher self first, to make sure they're aligned with the growth you really need, rather than just what you *want*. So, let's take a moment to brainstorm. Gather a piece of paper and writing implement or a nearby screen with a note-taking app. Get those ideas flowing.

Start off with physical goals just to get ideas out. What bodily healing goals do you have? Better joints? Easier digestion? Increased strength? Fewer allergies? Then, move on to your emotional goals if you have any (and the kundalini hopes you do!). What emotional growth do you hope to achieve? Increased empathy? More friends? A real, loving, intimate relationship? A change of pace in life? Finally, look at your spiritual goals. Are you hoping for increased psychic abilities? More spiritual friends or perhaps a guru or a teacher? Are you simply here to awaken your kundalini? What else is going on with you?

When you've been able to write out all the potential goals you have, see if there are any common themes throughout the list. If you've written a bodily goal of becoming stronger and an emotional goal of learning how to say "no" better," then your overall goals as a person (on all three bases: bodily, emotional, and spiritual) seem to align with increased strength. Focus on that when you perform these kundalini meditations and focus on the solar plexus as your "hot spot" or "trouble spot" for you need a little core work to get your energy flowing in tip-top shape once more.

Once you have all these hopes and goals written out and you've been able to define or pull out any themes or overall standards in your passage toward growth, you'll have a much better time establishing your chant or mantra. With that added verbal boost to your meditations as mentioned above, that kundalini snake will have added direction and the verve to get things done. Through just a touch of brainstorming, you'll enable your advancement to be faster, more thorough, and even more long-lasting.

IV: Visualizing & Making Space for Awakening

Let's get into the meat of this meditation now. With the information you've been provided with, you know what the kundalini is, how it works in the body, and what it wants to do for you. You've also assessed what it is you want for yourself and how to filter out desires that have lesser importance. Your familiarity with the kundalini will be increased exponentially now and forever more, for your awakening will be put fully underway in a matter of minutes.

If your overall awakening seems to take longer to play out in your life than you've hoped for, the most important thing is to be patient and understanding with yourself. In these cases, practice active and radical forgiveness, acceptance, and appreciation of yourself without any adjustments or energetic shifts. Sometimes the kundalini energy within us can tell we're forcing something and it will make us wait to realize that before it allows us to blossom. Sometimes we need to change our diets to become more receptive to this transformative energy. Sometimes we need to start practicing different meditations, different sports, or different activities in general to gather information first before the kundalini is ready to become engaged. Sometimes, we need to wait, and that's absolutely okay.

If you find yourself meeting a blockage in your development and awakening potential, take a step back and consider *why* this might be happening. Your ego may be a bit too loud. Your internal imbalances may be taking command. Your goals may not be as pure as you think. Simply take a step back and reevaluate. If everything seems on the up and up after your examination, keep up the good, meditative work, and the universe will surely respond in time. It'll just be more so on the *universe's* time, rather than your own.

When you're ready to move forward, see yourself in your own mind's eye. With those eyes closed and your breathing deep and steady, visualize yourself in your own imagination. See yourself sitting in that comfortable position, breathing deeply, and finding your peace. Note how strong and secure you look, how dedicated and how relaxed too. Then, see yourself surrounded by a powerful white light. This light seems to emanate from your skin and it glows like the sunrise. As this light fills the space around you, you feel certain of your higher nature and feel affirmed in your purpose with this guided meditation.

As you look at yourself sitting and breathing in peaceful meditation, make sure you are both sitting with strong posture to validate the work your core and spine are about to do. In real life and in your visualization, start to engage in your chant or mantra once more. Speak about what you want to attract into your life and what you will gain from your kundalini awakening. And visualize that the light becomes brighter around you with every repetition of your chant that you vocalize.

Promise yourself to the world. Promise to that world and to all Shakti surrounding you that you will say "yes" from now on as much as possible, for the sake of this divine connection. Promise yourself that you will do everything the universe points you towards, for you know that your process of awakening doesn't stop with these 5-to-10-minute meditations. Promise to devote yourself toward the generative, creative, and supportive force of the universe and feel that snake at the base of your spine starts stirring, start awakening its motion through your chakras.

As the snake awakens at your Root Chakra, visualize the light around you (that is the light around yourself in your imagination) turning bright red. See a smile grow on your face and intuitively feel that this imagined-self feels assured, protected and safe, and therefore happy. As the snake moves up to the Sacral Chakra, see that light turn deep and glowing orange. The smile lingers on your face, but you know that this time it's because you feel inspired and ready to create art after a long, long dry spell. Moving upward, the snake tickles your Solar Plexus Chakra and you laugh aloud as your surrounding light becomes yellow like sunshine. You know that your confidence and strength of will fueled that laugh rather than the serpent's tickle.

As the snake moves upward, it activates your Heart Chakra and your surrounding light becomes this brilliant shade of green. Your smile becomes deeper, a little wider, if that's even possible and you feel love exuding out in ripples even just through your imagination. Next, the serpent licks your Throat Chakra, turning your light a simple pale blue and your smile reflects ease of speech. You look like you could burst out into joyous song at any moment. Then, to your Third-Eye Chakra, the serpent coolly climbs, making your light shine deep indigo rays from your skin. Your smile suggests calm knowledge and insights gleaned through senses other than the standard 5, and finally, the snake swirls into and through the Crown Chakra, turning your surrounding light a peaceful and glorious purple. Your smile expresses truths divined from source energy and reminds of those often found on ascendant masters across time.

Now, visualize that the snake starts to move just a little faster. The colors of your surrounding light change much quicker too and before long, the snake's motion turns you into a rainbow blur of color. Eventually, with calm and collected breath on your part, the serpent begins to move so freely that the rainbow colors create a haze of simply pulsating white light. Feel the lights that surround you in your imagination being forced through the prism of sped-up time, revealing their true nature as pure white healing light all along. You were always working toward kundalini awakening, you just helped to speed up the process! The knowing, connected smile you see on your own face is constant and you sense that nothing can harm you. You know that awakening is nigh.

This awakening will follow you out into the real world where you're constantly posed with important and unspoken decisions. This awakening will encourage you to act differently and engage with others in completely new ways in support of the growth that's to come. In that case, you'll definitely want to say "yes" to anything that piques your interest or that serendipitously points you in line to your goals. Trust yourself, trust the universe. Keep your head on straight and breathe deeply. Your transformation is just around the corner!

V: What's to Come

In your process of kundalini awakening, there will be a handful of hard times and strange side effects. There will be glorious moments and there will be breakdowns. When you work to unlock this awareness of your internal energy spheres and their impact on your overall health, you will experience intense fluctuations before any sort of enlightenment can be reached. You might even find yourself changing and shifting in appetites, desires, and potential before you settle in your new self.

Awakening is always a big moment and it's not just good things that will happen to you – well, it's all for the good, but some of it might be uncomfortable. Awakening often involves detoxing as well, which can mean irrational, stinky, moody times ahead. During awakening, you might feel like your path is revealed more clearly or that you have a greater sense of direction, but you could also have to live through frustrated, listless, isolated, and directionless moments in order to get there.

When you awaken, you'll undeniably have a stronger sense of yourself, as you exist in this dimension, as well as how you exist on higher planes as a self (or soul) connected to God (or source energy). During your awakening, you will feel full of self, you will hear your inner voice more clearly, and you will feel overwhelmed with new direction and potential. When you're ready to get to this point, you will know, and once your awakening begins, you should have no doubts about what's happening inside of you.

As far as what you can expect in your kundalini awakening, let's start with the emotional complexities. Your breathing and consciousness now will help you feel less out of control in response to anxiety, stress, and frustrations later on. You will have increased sensations of openness, acceptance, purposefulness, and joy. You may even feel blissful more often than ever before. You may still have extremely low-energy days and you may still go through periods of intense sadness or depression, however, once full awakening is achieved, you will not be able to harbor these types of emotions for very much longer. You simply won't have space for them alongside all the rest of your abilities and strengths.

Emotionally, too, you'll become vibrant with buzzing energy and creative urges. You'll have rid yourself of any momentary blockages to any of your chakras so you'll be flooded with pure source energy at this time. You'll feel that something you've been longing for has been achieved and your aura will surely be affected. As you breathe in this moment, consider the future at your fingertips. Consider your chances at healing and energetic awakening and let yourself feel hope and confidence that these moments truly are coming. Through this conscious attraction, your meditation will create your new world.

In addition, when you're in the throes of kundalini awakening, you'll feel lingering traces of feelings and emotions from years and years ago as your body forces you to process what memories haven't fully healed in you yet. Your body will speak in volumes as you detoxify and develop yourself anew. You'll need to work through certain things to get into a full awakening, so if you find yourself spontaneously bursting into tears or having hot flashes, erratic outbursts, or angry tendencies, you're going to get through it. Remind yourself these things need to happen, they need to get out for you to be cleansed and opened to the universe.

Now, let's look at some of the physical side effects that you may experience during this awakening process. At first, you'll likely get energetic ripples through your system that feels something similar to anxiety. While your energy is getting rewired and repatterned into a healthier consciousness and vibration, the shift can be intense. Seek alone time to tune into your inner vibration and use meditations like these to help that shift feel as effortless as possible.

In this moment, where you've found your peace and where you create your future, you breathe and establish your space. At this moment, you awaken the snake of energy within you who comes to dance up through your chakras to your crown and back down to your core. At this moment, you invite awakening and you accept all that's to come. The energetic shifts, the changes in diet and craving, the changes in interest, the overwhelmed feelings, the need to dance or run, the need to slow down and exactly what it is that you really need – these things and more come your way with your practice of clearing and intensifying your power.

Finally, let's see what your end-goal may look like once your awakening is complete. Breathe with the flow of the facts coming your way and feel relieved, warmed, strong, and hopeful about their enactment in your life in the near future. You will know your inner voice well and you'll trust its insights whenever you hear it, for you know this voice connects you to a higher self or guardian of some sort. With the kundalini energy awakened, you will be this connected. You will also have a deep connection to your inner Truth. So many theories of life and world today reject concepts like "truth with a capital T," but the enlightened, awakened individual is earnestly able to tap into their personal truth, the truth attached to their soul and through this connection, they can come to heal any ancestral, personal, or past life ailments that might be appearing in their current self-expression.

With the kundalini awakened, the individual will experience something like a second puberty that unlocks authenticity, wisdom, bliss, and more once the excess is sloughed away. Through quiet, meditative alone time, you will be rejuvenated and inspired to continue. You will come to a place of acceptance and appreciation of your new found gifts and will find emotional obstacles cleared away.

At the final stage of awakening, you will lose touch with the importance of ego-driven things and ways of being. Your pure state of being – as energy – will be the only one of value and the all-demanding, all-distracting "I" that you were will fade away as you realize how connected you are to everything and everyone around you. As you reach the climax of your kundalini awakening, as that snake reaches its fullest ease of movement within you, you will feel yourself becoming One with all that is. Through love, devotion, and practice, you will transcend. You will blossom.

Thank you!

Before you go, I just wanted to say thank you for purchasing my book.

You could have picked from dozens of other books on the same topic but you took a chance and chose this one.

So, a HUGE thanks to you for getting this book and for reading all the way to the end.

Now I wanted to ask you for a small favor. **Could you please consider posting a review on the platform? Reviews are one of the easiest ways to support the work of independent authors.**

This feedback will help me continue to write the type of books that will help you get the results you want. So if you enjoyed it, please let me know! (-:

Printed in Great Britain
by Amazon